JOHN TERRY

FOOTBALL ALL-STARS

RORY CALLAN

John Terry is a tough, world-class footballer. Read all about his club and international football career inside – then flip over to find out more about Rio Ferdinand.

EDGE

FRANKLIN WATTS

LONDON·SYDNEY

First published in 2012 by
Franklin Watts
338 Euston Road
London NW1 3BH

Franklin Watts Australia
Level 17/207 Kent Street
Sydney NSW 2000

Text copyright © Rory Callan 2012
Design © Franklin Watts 2012

Series editor: Adrian Cole
Art director: Jonathan Hair
Design: Steve Prosser
Picture research: Diana Morris

A CIP catalogue record of this book
is available from the British Library.

ISBN: 978 1 4451 0210 8

Dewey classification: 796.3'34'092

Printed in China.

Franklin Watts is a division of
Hachette Children's Books,
an Hachette UK company.
www.hachette.co.uk

Acknowledgements:
Giuliano Bevilacqua/Rex Features: XV.
Steve Butler/Actionplus: back cover, 12.
Graham Chadewick/Daily Mail/Rex
Features: 19. Thomas Coex/AFP/Getty
Images: 18. Kevork Djansezian/Getty
Images: 21. Francis Gibbery/Chelsea
FC via Getty Images: 7. David Giles/PA
Archive/PAI: VII. Tom Hevezi/AP/PAI: V.
Tommy Hindley/Professional Sport/Topfoto:
9. Andy Hooper/Daily Mail/Rex Features:
IX. Owen Humphries/PA Archive/PAI: 20.
David Klein/Professional Sport/Topfoto:
15, 17, XXI. Charles Knight/Rex Features:
13. Alex Livesey /Getty Images: XI, XIX.
Popperfoto/Getty Images: 5. Ben Radford
/Corbis: front cover. RIA Novosti/Topfoto:
XII. Clive Rose/Getty Images: 23. Neal
Simpson/Empics/PAI: XVII. Darren Walsh/
Chelsea FC via Getty Images: 11. Kirsty
Wigglesworth/AP/PAI: XXII.

Every attempt has been made to clear
copyright. Should there be any inadvertent
omission please apply to the publisher for
rectification.

Note: At the time of going to press, the
statistics in this book were up to date.
However, due to the nature of sport, it is
possible that some of these may now be
out of date.

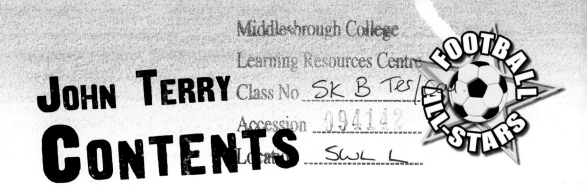

JOHN TERRY
CONTENTS

KING JOHN 4

EARLY DAYS 6

CHELSEA CAPTAIN
AND LEAGUE WINNER 8

COURAGE UNDER FIRE 10

CHELSEA LEGEND 12

WORLD CUP 2006 14

ENGLAND CAPTAIN 18

WORLD CUP 2010 20

TIMELINE, GLOSSARY AND INDEX 24

KING JOHN

**2004 European Championships qualifier,
Turkey vs England, 11 October 2003, Istanbul, Turkey**

6:30pm, 45 minutes before kickoff

The England team is in Istanbul for the final Euro 2004 **qualifying game** with Turkey. They have to secure at least a draw to qualify, while Turkey need a win to finish top of the group.

England's away dressing room is cold and cramped. The players can feel the stadium shake as the Turkey fans jump up and down in the stand above them. John Terry puts on his number 5 shirt. At the age of 22, this is only his fourth start for England.

37 minutes

After 37 minutes, it's still 0–0, when England are awarded a penalty. David Beckham shoots, but the ball whizzes over. The whistles and jeers of the Turkey supporters are louder than ever. Turkey, sensing they've had a lucky escape, begin to pile on the pressure. Just before half time one of the Turkey **midfielders** shoots from 25 yards out. The ball is on its way into the net just as Terry throws his body in the way to make a crucial **block**.

45 minutes – half time

As players leave the pitch, a mass brawl breaks out in the tunnel. Around 50 players and officials from both sides are involved. Terry wades in to protect his teammates. It takes several minutes to break it up.

▶ *John Terry works hard for England in 2003, when they played Turkey.*

Second half

From the start of the second half, Turkey throw everything they have at the England goal. Terry blocks, heads and tackles as if his life depends on it. No matter what Turkey do, they can't get past the England defence.

90 minutes – full time

Thanks to Terry's bravery, England secure the draw they need and head to the European Championships. The England players celebrate by dancing arm in arm around the centre circle.

Terry is exhausted but thrilled. People back home are impressed with his performance. One newspaper headline the next day reads: "King John Saves England!" ***But how did he get there?***

John George Terry was born on 7 December 1980, and grew up in Barking, east London. His dad, Ted Terry, played with local pub football teams as Terry was growing up. He watched his dad play at the weekends and was surrounded by the tough tackling, passion and "never say die" attitude of British football.

Chelsea school boy

Terry spent all his time either playing or talking about football. In 1994, Chelsea Football Club (FC) asked Terry to join their youth training team and he jumped at the chance. After a few weeks the training ground at Chelsea began to feel like his second home. The coaching was excellent and he was well looked after.

School-boy contract

When the club offered him a two year school-boy **contract**, he was delighted to accept it. He was just 14, and even though he didn't know it at the time, in four years he would be **lining out** in the Chelsea first team.

▶ *Terry poses for a photograph in his Chelsea strip during the 1998/99 football season.*

CHELSEA CAPTAIN AND LEAGUE WINNER

During the summer of 2003, the Russian billionaire, Roman Abramovich, bought Chelsea FC. With one of the wealthiest men in the world now owning the club, there was plenty of money available for new players. Abramovich said that he wanted Chelsea to become one of the biggest clubs in the world, and he was prepared to use his money to make it happen.

Chelsea club captain

At the same time, Jose Mourinho, one of the most talented young managers in Europe, was appointed as Chelsea's manager. After only three days of looking at his new squad, Mourinho knew Terry was the natural leader of the team. Before travelling to the USA for a pre-season tour, he asked Terry to be club captain. Terry couldn't believe it – never in his wildest dreams did he think he would become captain of Chelsea. Mourinho said that the captain's armband was well deserved:

"JT is an inspirational player for us, he makes you want to be a winner."

Premier League champions

Chelsea played brilliantly in Terry's first year as captain. By Christmas in the 2004/05 season, Chelsea had built up a commanding lead at the top of the table. They went on to be crowned Premier League champions. Chelsea fans celebrated when the trophy was presented to Terry and the team. He became the second player in the history of Chelsea to captain the club to a League victory. The year ended perfectly for Terry when he was awarded the highest honour a professional footballer can get – the PFA Player of the Year.

▲ *Terry wearing the captain's armband for Chelsea in 2004.*

9

COURAGE UNDER FIRE

Chelsea won the Premier League title again in 2005/06, but Terry suffered a serious back injury early in the 2006/07 season. It put him out for over three months. He returned to the team to play against Arsenal in the 2007 Carling Cup Final. If anyone ever doubted Terry's toughness, they certainly didn't after this game. When he dived in for a header, he was kicked in the face and knocked unconscious. He was rushed to hospital, where the doctors insisted that he stay overnight. Instead, Terry went back to the stadium to celebrate Chelsea's win with his teammates!

Tough performances

Later that season, Chelsea squared up to their league rivals, Manchester United. After seven minutes of the match, Terry was tackled heavily by Wayne Rooney. Terry's leg began to swell up, but he wouldn't come off the pitch, even though the **physios** urged him to. After the game he had to have 10 stitches in his leg. ***"There was no way I was coming off,"*** he said after the game. Chelsea had gone two full years without defeat at Stamford Bridge thanks to performances like this from Terry.

Lucky captain

In 2008, Terry dislocated his elbow during the last game of the League season, and was taken to hospital. With the Champions League final in four days, Chelsea looked as though they were going to be without their captain. Luckily, on the way to the hospital his elbow was popped back into place and the next morning he declared himself fit to play.

▲ *Terry is stretchered off during the Champions League in 2008.*

CHELSEA LEGEND

In 2009, Chelsea appointed a new manager, Carlo Ancelotti. He introduced an attacking style of play. Terry liked Ancelotti's training methods and positive approach to the game, while Ancelotti was full of praise for Terry. In his very first interview as Chelsea manager, he said that Terry was one of the world's greatest defenders and should continue as club captain.

Premier League winners 2009/10

During the 2009/10 season, all of Chelsea's top players – Terry, Frank Lampard, Didier Drogba and Nicolas Anelka, hit top form. They played exciting, attacking football, and won the Premier League, finishing one point ahead

▲ Terry attacks the ball in the air to win a header.

of arch rivals Manchester United. On the last day of the season they thrashed Wigan Athletic 8–0 at Stamford Bridge, taking their goals scored to 103 – a new Premier League record.

FA Cup victory

One week later, Terry led Chelsea to victory in the FA Cup Final, with a 1–0 win over Portsmouth. When Terry received the cup from Prince William, the FA President, he sealed his place as a Chelsea legend by becoming the first person to captain the team to the Premier League and FA Cup "double".

Lap of honour

Terry applauded the Chelsea fans as he led his team on a lap of honour around the Wembley pitch. Terry saluted the supporters to thank them for their loyalty.

▲ *Terry and his Chelsea teammates celebrate winning the Premier League and FA Cup double in 2009/10 with a ride on an open-top bus.*

WORLD CUP 2006

Terry's first appearance for the senior England team was in 2003, when they played Serbia and Montenegro, beating them 3–1. When Terry was selected for the World Cup 2006 England **squad**, he was playing the best football of his life. He was willing to give his all for England in the World Cup:

"If I'm selected I will sweat blood and tears for the cause."

A nervous start

England won their first two games in the competition as expected. However the 1–0 victory over Paraguay, and the 2–0 win over Trinidad and Tobago (who were ranked 57th in the world) were not good performances. England faced Sweden in the last group match, needing a draw to finish top of the group. With one minute left to play, England were leading 2–1. Sweden pushed the ball forward in one last attack. Terry failed to clear the ball out of the penalty box, allowing Sweden striker, Henrik Larsson, to score. The game finished 2–2. It wasn't Terry's best performance in an England shirt, but as he said after the game:

"We've finished top of the group and we can't do much more than that."

England were four games away from winning the World Cup.

▶ *Terry clears the ball from the England defence during their match against Trinidad and Tobago at the World Cup 2006.*

World Cup knockout stages, 2006

Terry put this poor performance behind him and focused on the first-round knockout game against Ecuador. England won 1–0 with Terry putting in a man-of-the-match performance.

England vs Portugal, 2006

In the **quarter-final** against Portugal, England played some brilliant football in the first half, but failed to score. Then in the second half, when Wayne Rooney was sent off in the 62nd minute, the whole game changed. England were down to ten men against a highly skillful Portugal team. England had to defend and Terry played superbly, leading the back four. He helped to stop Portugal scoring through the rest of the second half and extra time.

Penalty shootout

The match went to penalties. The England players were exhausted. They had been down to ten men for almost an hour in the 30-degree Celsius heat. England lost the **penalty shoot-out** and were sent crashing out of the tournament. Terry was in tears after the game. He had given all of his energy, but unfortunately it just wasn't enough.

After his outstanding displays in the World Cup, Terry was the only England player to be named on the FIFA World Cup Team of the Tournament. Terry was now at the very top of his profession. If football fans around the world did not know his name before the World Cup, then they certainly knew it afterwards. At the age of 24, the lad from Barking in east London was now a world-wide superstar.

▶ *Terry can't hide his emotions after England are beaten on penalties by Portugal during the World Cup 2006 quarter-finals.*

ENGLAND CAPTAIN

In 2006, when Steve McClaren became manager of England, he made John Terry the team captain. In the press conference after the appointment, Terry said he was:

"...very proud to be given this honour, being captain of England is an incredible challenge and one that I'm really looking forward to."

Terry's first job as England captain was to help set up the *Team England Footballers' Charity*. England players now donate their international match fees to the charity and players also go to fund-raising events. Every year £1 million is raised.

▲ *Terry listens carefully to Fabio Capello's instructions during training.*

In June 2008, Fabio Capello was appointed England manager. He waited before choosing a permanent captain for the 2010 World Cup qualifying campaign. He wanted to see who would be the best leader of the team.

Capello decided to make Terry his permanent England captain. He said that Terry had a *"big personality and the right attitude for the job"*.

▲ *Fabio Capello and John Terry at the press conference to announce that Terry will be the permanent England captain.*

Difficult times

However, just 17 months later, Terry had lost the most important position in English football. After **allegations** about his private life, Terry's photograph was splashed all over the news. Fabio Capello was afraid that the bad **publicity** would have a negative effect on England's preparations for the World Cup. He called a meeting with Terry and told him that he was taking the England captaincy away from him. It was devastating news for Terry, but he accepted the manager's decision, and vowed to do his best for England in the World Cup.

WORLD CUP 2010

After captaining Chelsea to another Premier League title and FA Cup trophy, Terry was in good spirits heading to the World Cup in South Africa.

World Cup training camp

Seven days after lifting the FA Cup at Wembley, Terry travelled with his England teammates to their World Cup training camp in Austria. The training conditions were tough, with lots of hard work. Players were not allowed to use mobile phones and they had to do extra gym work every day. Terry found it hard work after a long season with Chelsea.

When England landed in South Africa, they began studying video footage of their Group C opponents: USA, Algeria and Slovenia.

▶ *Terry and his England teammates warm up for a practice session.*

Group C games

England's opening group game against the USA got off to a perfect start when Steven Gerrard scored after only 4 minutes of play. England controlled the game well until 5 minutes before half time when goalkeeper, Robert Green, made a terrible mistake. A tame shot from striker, Clint Dempsey spilled through Green's gloves and went into the England goal. From then until the end of the game it was the USA who were on top, and the game ended 1–1.

▶ *Terry heads the ball away as the USA press forward during their Group C game.*

Six days later England took on Algeria, supposedly the weakest team in the group, but the game was drawn 0–0.

With only 2 points from their opening games, England had to win the final group game against Slovenia to progress to the last 16 of the competition. With 30,000 of their loyal but nervous supporters in the stadium, England put in a commanding first half performance. Jermain Defoe scored in the first half to make it 1–0 to England, but then as the match went on, England began to lose possession. Slovenia would certainly have scored but for two crucial tackles from Terry in the dying minutes of the match. When the referee blew the final whistle, Terry and his teammates celebrated. It was their first victory in South Africa.

World Cup knockout stage

England were drawn against Germany for the last 16 knockout phase. There was a confident mood in the England squad leading up to the game. But Germany put on a world-class performance and defeated England 4–1.

▶ *Terry presses Germany's Mesut Özil in the knockout stage of World Cup 2010.*

England EURO 2012 Group G qualifying

In March 2011, Fabio Capello decided to give the captain's armband back to Terry, who was delighted to get a second chance. He led the England football team through the qualifying stages of the European Championships.

Ashley Cole, Chris Smalling, Gary Cahill and John Terry formed the defence for England against Bulgaria in Sofia. The strong first half performance was enough to kill off the game, and England walked away with a 3–0 victory. Terry said after the game:

"It was a good performance and a great win."

His tough performances helped England to qualify for the EURO 2012 tournament in September 2011. And with Terry at the heart of defence, everyone has high hopes for the future. As younger players start to push into the national team, his experience will be really important. After qualifying, Terry said:

"It's a great thing to get where we've got, we're top and we've worked hard all the way through."

ENGLAND CAPTAIN

Three months before the 2010 World Cup, Ferdinand received the greatest honour of his career, when Fabio Capello appointed him as the England team captain. Ferdinand also had the honour of being the first black player to captain England at the World Cup.

Ferdinand took his role seriously, making sure that every player in the squad felt comfortable and relaxed. He was especially aware of making the younger players feel like part of the team. He was hoping that South Africa 2010 would be third time lucky.

A captain's shattered dream

In fact, Ferdinand's World Cup dream ended during England's very first training session. He collided with striker Emile Heskey and hit the ground hard. When he got back on his feet, he was limping heavily. Later, in hospital, scans showed that he had damaged ligaments in his left knee. The doctors had to break the news to Ferdinand that his World Cup was over.

Ferdinand took the news calmly. He was obviously upset that his chance to captain England in a World Cup match was gone, but he was experienced enough to know that injury is a part of life for a professional footballer.

Injury continued to affect Ferdinand's fitness in 2010 and 2011, but with his strength and determination, Ferdinand remains one of the best centre-backs in the world.

◀ *Ferdinand on crutches after he was injured during a training session. The injury put him out of World Cup 2010.*

TIMELINE GLOSSARY

Team	Appearances	Goals
League		
1996–2000 West Ham United	127	2
1996–1997 Bournemouth (loan)	10	0
2000–2002 Leeds United	54	2
2002– Manchester United	244	6
National		
1996–1997 England U–18	7	0
1997–2000 England U–21	5	0
1997– England	81	3

Caps The word used in sport to show that the player represented their national team.

Centre-back A defender who plays in the middle of defence.

Council estate A number of houses built by the local council and rented to families on lower incomes.

Debut First appearance, in this case as a player in a particular team.

Penalty shoot-out In the event of a draw, players from each team take it in turns to score goals from the penalty spot.

Physios Short for physiotherapists; people trained to treat injuries or illnesses through massage and exercises.

Quarter-finals Eight teams compete in the quarter-finals in order to win a place in the semi-finals.

Squad In football, the small group of players which makes up the team and the substitutes.

Trials Events where footballers play matches and do training exercises, watched by managers or other key people who will be looking out for the most talented players.

UEFA Union of European Football Associations.

INDEX

Argentina (national team) XVIII

ballet VI
Barcelona FC XIV
Brazil (national team) XVIII, XIX

Capello, Fabio XXIII
Champions League XII–XV
Charlton, Sir Bobby XVI
Chelsea FC VIII, XIII, XIV, XV

Denmark (national team) XVIII
Drogba, Didier XII, XIII, XIV

England (national team) IV, V, VI, VII, VIII, XVI–XXIII
   captain of IV, V, XXIII

Ferguson, Sir Alex X

injuries XXIII

Leeds United FC X

Manchester United FC X–XV
   captain of X–XV
Mexico (national team) IV, V

Portugal (national team) XX, XXI
Premier League VIII, X, XVI

Redknapp, Harry VIII
Rivaldo XVIII, XIX
Ronaldo, Cristiano XIII, XXI

West Ham United FC VIII, IX
World Cup 1998 XVI, XVIII
World Cup 2002 XVI, XVIII
World Cup 2006 XVI, XX, XXI
World Cup 2010 IV, V, XVI, XXII, XXIII

TIMELINE GLOSSARY

Team	Appearances	Goals
League		
1998– Chelsea	349	23
2000 Nottingham Forest (loan)	6	0
National		
2000–2002 England U–21	9	1
2003– England	71	6

Allegations When statements or stories are made about someone or something, not always backed up by facts.

Block When a footballer uses his or her body to stop the ball from moving forward.

Contract An agreement.

Lining out When a team lines up and walks out onto the pitch at the beginning of a match.

Midfielder A player who plays mostly in the mid section of the football pitch.

Penalty shoot-out In the event of a draw, players from each team take it in turns to score goals from the penalty spot.

Physios Short for physiotherapists; people trained to treat injuries or illnesses through massage and exercises.

Publicity Drawing attention to something or someone by releasing information in the form of adverts, press releases, newspaper articles and public appearances.

Qualifying game The match that decides which team will win a place in a further competition.

Quarter-finals Eight teams compete in the quarter-finals in order to win a place in the semi-finals.

Squad In football, the small group of players which makes up the team and the substitutes.

INDEX

Abramovich, Roman 8
Algeria (national team) 20, 21
Ancelotti, Carlo 12

Bulgaria (national team) 22

Capello, Fabio 18, 19, 22
Champions League 10, 11
Chelsea FC 6–13, 20
    captain of 8–13, 20

Ecuador (national team) 15
England (national team) 4, 5, 14–23
    captain of 18–19, 22
European Championships 4, 5, 22

FA Cup Final 13, 20

Germany (national team) 22

injuries 10, 11

Manchester United FC 10, 12
McClaren, Steve 18
Mourinho, José 8

Paraguay (national team) 14
PFA Player of the Year 9
Portsmouth FC 13
Portugal (national team) 16, 17
Premier League 8, 9, 10, 12, 13, 20

Rooney, Wayne 10, 16

Serbia and Montenegro (national team) 14
Slovenia (national team) 20, 21
Sweden (national team) 14

Team England Footballers' Charity 18
Trinidad and Tobego (national team) 14, 15
Turkey (national team) 4, 5

USA (national team) 20, 21

World Cup 2006 14–17
World Cup 2010 18–23

▲ Portugal's Cristiano Ronaldo and Helder Postiga beat England's
Rio Ferdinand to the ball.

Germany 2006

Before heading to the 2006 World Cup in Germany, Ferdinand felt England were in a strong position to win the tournament. England would be playing in a European country, with matches played in the evening, meaning the temperatures wouldn't be too high. England also had one of the strongest squads in the world. This was England's best chance to win the World Cup since 1966. Before the tournament, Ferdinand said:

"I like the pressure. I love when there is pressure to do well and to achieve things, to go out and perform – but everyone's different."

World Cup Finals, quarter-final knockout stage

By the time they lined out against Portugal in the quarter-final, England had already played four games and had conceded only two goals. The England vs Portugal match started cautiously – with few scoring chances. Then Wayne Rooney was sent off early in the second half. With the extra man, Portugal took control of the ball and bombarded the England defence.

Ferdinand was determined to do anything to stop Portugal from scoring. He threw himself in front of shots, headed the ball away and put in some perfectly timed last gasp tackles. His grit and determination stopped the Portuguese from scoring and the match finished 0–0 after extra time.

Unfortunately for England, they lost 3–1 on penalties. After the defeat, Ferdinand was upset. He couldn't hold back the tears.

However, Brazil's star player, Ronaldinho, had other ideas. He set up Rivaldo for Brazil's equaliser, then scored an extraordinary goal with a shot from 35 yards out to give Brazil a 2–1 lead. In the last 15 minutes, England tried to grab a second goal, but Brazil held on to their lead, and England were out.

WORLD CUP WARRIOR

France 1998

Ferdinand didn't actually play in this tournament, but the experience shaped his future international career. He lived and trained with England's best players, and saw what was needed to play at a World Cup level. Ferdinand learned that everything at a World Cup match is bigger. The crowds were louder, the media attention was intense, the players were under enormous pressure to perform and every one had to be focused. Ferdinand said:

"You just concentrate on playing and then deal with the outcome later. I switch straight off."

Japan and Korea 2002

By the time Ferdinand went to Japan and Korea in 2002, he was ready for action. His performances throughout the tournament were outstanding. By the end of the competition the newspapers were describing Ferdinand as a "world-class" defender.

England conceded just one goal in their first four matches, which included a 1–0 victory over Argentina and a 3–0 hammering of Denmark. Having cruised into the **quarter-finals**, England now faced a meeting with World Cup superpower, Brazil. The game was played in sweltering 35-degree heat, and after Michael Owen scored the opening goal, Ferdinand began to believe that England could win.

▶ *Brazil's Rivaldo comes up against tough-tackling Ferdinand in the England defence during the World Cup quarter-finals in 2002.*

ENGLAND VETERAN

Ferdinand has over 80 international **caps**, and has been in the England squad at four FIFA World Cup tournaments: France 1998, Japan and Korea 2002, Germany 2006 and South Africa 2010. Sir Bobby Charlton, a World Cup winner and one of the best players of all time, is the only other England player to have been selected for four World Cup squads. Ferdinand's defensive skills and superb physical fitness have helped him to stay at the heart of the England defence.

Off to a shaky start

With all of this success you might think that Ferdinand was an England natural from the beginning – but he wasn't. In fact, his England career got off to a shaky start. He was invited to **trials** for the England Under-15 and Under-16 teams. However, he didn't get on very well at the trials. He was young and very nervous, and this affected his performances.

England debut

Soon after this things improved for Ferdinand. He grew by about 12 centimetres in height, so by the time he was 18 years old he was 1.83 metres tall and physically strong. He was ready to defend against the best players in the Premier League. The week after his 19th birthday, Ferdinand received the best present a young footballer could ever dream of: he made his England international debut in a friendly game against Cameroon.

▶ *Rio Ferdinand shouts instructions during his first England game in 1997.*

▼ Ferdinand holds up the UEFA Champions League trophy with teammate Ryan Giggs after Manchester United defeated Chelsea in the 2008 Final.

UEFA Champions League Final, 2008 – second half

The United defence managed to soak up the waves of Chelsea attacks after half time. Ferdinand had to use all of his physical strength to stop Chelsea's two imposing strikers – Didier Drogba and Nicolas Anelka – from scoring. Ferdinand was a rock in the United defence, and remained calm despite the pressure.

Extra time and penalties

After a tense period of extra time, the game remained tied at 1–1 and went to penalties. Manchester United won the **penalty shoot-out** 6–5; now they were officially the best team in Europe! Ferdinand received the Champions League trophy, becoming only the third player in the history of Manchester United to do so. He raised the cup to the cheers of his teammates and supporters. It was an emotional few moments for him. As a child, Ferdinand could never have dreamed that one day he would be captain of a Champions League-winning team.

Facing off against Barcelona

Ferdinand was lucky enough to be in the Manchester United squad in the 2009 and 2011 Champions League finals. In both games they came up against Spanish champions, Barcelona, and lost 2–0 in 2009, and 3–1 in 2011. Ferdinand can be proud of his European record though. To play in three Champions League finals in four years was an incredible achievement. After the defeat against Barcelona in 2009, Ferdinand recalled:

"Beating Chelsea in Moscow was a great experience, but the memories of losing to Barcelona in Rome 12 months later are far more vivid."

Cu..Quering Europe

Playing at Manchester United gave Ferdinand the chance to play in the Champions League regularly. Ferdinand loved the challenge of testing himself against the best strikers in the world. But what he really wanted was to win:

"Winning the Champions League has to have a bearing [on how great your team is]. Teams who are considered great have normally managed to win the European Cup."

UEFA Champions League Final, 2008 – first half

The stadium floodlights were on, and the fans were cheering wildly. This was how the Luzhniki Stadium in Moscow appeared on the most important night of Ferdinand's club career to date. Manchester United were in Russia to take on Chelsea in the **UEFA** Champions League Final, 2008. Ferdinand was the Manchester United captain. This was his once in a lifetime chance of lifting the most important trophy in European club football.

It was one of the most intense and exciting European finals of all time. In true English style, the game was played at a fast pace from start to finish, with both sets of players throwing themselves into every tackle. Manchester United opened the scoring through a well taken Cristiano Ronaldo goal after 26 minutes. Then Frank Lampard equalised for Chelsea before half time as Chelsea piled the pressure on United's defence.

◀ *Ferdinand leaps above Chelsea's Didier Drogba during the 2008 Champions League Final.*

MOVING ON UP

By the time Ferdinand was 21, he was a rising star in the Premier League. He moved to Leeds United for a record breaking fee of £18 million. He spent two successful seasons at Leeds, and was made captain in his second year at the club. Ferdinand was brilliant in the air, put in crunching tackles on opponents and had the gift of being able to set up attacks with sharp, accurate passes from defence. What made him extra special was his relaxed style of play; Ferdinand made defending at **centre-back** look easy, he was calm and in control – a real sign of a top-class player.

Manchester United

Ferdinand was so good that Sir Alex Ferguson, the manager of Manchester United, signed him for what was a record transfer fee of £30 million. Ferdinand couldn't believe his luck. As a kid his ambition had been to play in the Premier League, and now he was going to play for Britain's biggest club with an estimated 80 million fans around the world.

A world-class team

Manchester United was even better than Ferdinand had hoped. Every day in training he learnt from great players, sometimes just by watching their movement and positioning. The training facilities, and the medical and **physio** teams, were the best in the world. Plus, he also had Sir Alex Ferguson as his manager. The whole setup was a recipe for success. Ferdinand was determined to work hard and play to his full potential.

▶ *Ferdinand and Sir Alex Ferguson pose for press cameras after the player signed for Manchester United in 2002.*

WEST HAM UNITED

By the time he was 15, Ferdinand was wanted by nearly every club in London. He could have signed for Chelsea, Charlton, Millwall or QPR, but he decided to join West Ham United. Ferdinand liked the atmosphere at the club, and his mum and dad were happy that he would be well looked after. West Ham had struck a good deal too. Ferdinand's awareness, his physical size and strength, and his tackling ability were all excellent. His talent impressed West Ham's boss, Harry Redknapp, who could see in Ferdinand not just a future Premier League player, but a kid with the chance of making the England team.

Solid centre-back

Ferdinand made his Premier League **debut** aged just 17 years and 6 months. He quickly established himself as West Ham's number-one centre-back. Just a few months later, he was selected to train with the England **squad**. It is rare for an 18-year-old defender to make it into a national squad. Most international defenders make their debuts in their early to mid twenties. Ferdinand's selection for Euro '96 showed he had something special about him.

▶ *Ferdinand training with West Ham in 1998.*

LONDON BUY

Rio Ferdinand was born on 7 November, 1978. He grew up on a council estate in the heart of Peckham, in south-east London. The green area in front of his block of flats was perfect for playing football, and he played there with kids of all ages and nationalities from around the estate. Often, there could be 15 players from age 8 to 18 on each team, and the games would go on for 4 or 5 hours. Peckham was a poor area, with a lot of drug-dealing, theft and violence. So football was a perfect way for Ferdinand to use his energy in a positive way and stay out of trouble. Playing against older boys also improved his game as he had to use his skill, rather than strength, to get the ball past them.

Hidden talents

Although Ferdinand was passionate about football, he had other hobbies. He loved gymnastics and had quite a talent for it. He could, for example, do the back flip five or six times in a row! He also took up an unusual hobby for a future professional footballer – ballet dancing.

When he was 10 years old, Ferdinand won a scholarship to the Central School of Ballet in London. He travelled to central London for ballet lessons every week, for four years. He eventually gave it up at 14 to concentrate on football, but Ferdinand has always credited ballet for giving him improved balance, calmness and movement on the football pitch.

▶ *Ferdinand on the right of his England teammate Paul Gascoigne in 1997. They are part of the England side preparing to meet Moldova.*

attack eases and England take control of the game once more. After 35 minutes, Peter Crouch scores to put England 2–0 up.

9:50 pm (Full time)

Full time and the England players congratulate each other after a solid 3–1 victory. Led by Ferdinand, the players applaud the England fans. After a long, hard season the players are at last ready to fly out to South Africa for the adventure of a lifetime – to play in the World Cup Finals!

After the match Ferdinand says he is pleased with the team performance and is confident that the players can do the nation proud in South Africa. His comments will be broadcast all over the world and printed in newspapers and magazines on every continent. Everyone wants to know what the England captain has to say. **But how did he get there?**

▲ Rio Ferdinand congratulates his teammates after the England game against Mexico at Wembley Stadium in London.

ENGLAND'S COOL CAPTAIN

England vs Mexico – 24 May 2010, Wembley Stadium, London, England.
7:45 pm (15 minutes before kick off)

England are up against Mexico in their final home game before the 2010 World Cup in South Africa. The 88,638 England fans inside the new Wembley Stadium are ready to give their team a good send off. In the England dressing room, Rio Ferdinand prepares to lead his teammates into the player's tunnel. It's his 78th time playing for England, but tonight he is wearing the captain's armband for the first time.

7:52 pm (8 minutes before kick off)

As the first notes of *God Save the Queen* are played, the whole of Wembley sings with one voice. Ferdinand sings the anthem with passion – just 17 kilometres across the city, Ferdinand grew up on a **council estate** in south-east London dreaming of one day playing at Wembley.

8:22 pm (midway through the first half)

England are leading 1–0 already, but are coming under pressure from Mexico. It's time for Ferdinand to do what he does best – organise the defence and stop the opposition attackers from scoring. Ferdinand doesn't need to bark orders at his teammates; he simply gives the instructions and the others follow his command. With a few clean tackles from Ferdinand, the Mexico

Rio Ferdinand
Contents

ENGLAND'S COOL CAPTAIN   IV

LONDON BOY   VI

WEST HAM UNITED   VIII

MOVING ON UP   X

CONQUERING EUROPE   XIII

ENGLAND VETERAN   XVI

WORLD CUP WARRIOR   XVIII

GERMANY 2006   XX

ENGLAND CAPTAIN   XXIII

TIMELINE, GLOSSARY AND INDEX   XXIV

First published in 2012 by
Franklin Watts
338 Euston Road
London NW1 3BH

Franklin Watts Australia
Level 17/207 Kent Street
Sydney NSW 2000

Series editor: Adrian Cole
Art director: Jonathan Hair
Design: Steve Prosser
Picture research: Diana Morris

A CIP catalogue record of this book
is available from the British Library.

ISBN: 978 1 4451 0210 8

Dewey classification: 796.3'34'092

Printed in China.

Franklin Watts is a division of
Hachette Children's Books,
an Hachette UK company.
www.hachette.co.uk

RIO FERDINAND

FOOTBALL ALL-STARS

Rio Ferdinand is
one of the top
defenders in the
world. Read all
about his club
and international
football career
inside – then flip
over to find
out more about
John Terry.

EDGE
W FRANKLIN WATTS

LONDON·SYDNEY

RORY CALLAN